5 - Minute Miracles

5-Minute Miracles

Praying for People
with Simplicity and Power

" . . . where two or three come together in my name,
there am I with them" (Mt 18:20).

LINDA SCHUBERT

Resurrection Press
Mineola • New York

All scripture quotes are from the New International Version.

First published in 1993 by Resurrection Press, Ltd.
                        P.O. Box 248
                        Williston Park, NY 11596

Second Printing — January 1994
Third Printing — September 1994
Fourth Printing — August 1995
Fifth Printing — April 1996

ISBN 1-878718-08-8

Cover design by John Murello

Printed in the United States of America.

Dedication

This book is dedicated to the late Rev. Joseph A. Otte, C.PP.S., who was one of the people who introduced me to "5-minute miracles." In the cover photo, he was praying for me and giving me a word of encouragement. He spent many years in a healing ministry, teaching and encouraging people to pray with each other. "The Holy Spirit is in you," he would say. "You don't need me to pray. You do it." He instilled in us a faith that God could use us. In his later years he never let the Parkinson's disease that ravaged his body tame his free spirit or hold him back from speaking a healing word. If he were here today advising me on this book, he would encourage me extravagantly then probably instruct me to "Keep it simple." I will try to follow that unspoken advice.

The following quote is taken from a tribute booklet prepared for his jubilee celebration: "Father Joe, may the Lord always walk with you and may you rise to heaven with at least a small army of souls like mine that you have touched, inspired to holiness and nudged gently onto the straight and narrow but only safe path of Jesus." It is my prayer that each of us may have that said about us when it is our turn to go home to the Lord.

Contents

1

People are Hurting

"Since it is proper to the layman's state in life to spend his days in the midst of the world of secular transactions, he is called by God to burn with the Spirit of Christ and to exercise his apostolate in the world as a kind of leaven."

— Documents of Vatican II, Decree on
the Apostolate of the Laity, Chapter 1, paragraph 3

Theme: EVANGELIZATION (bringing the Good News): *"Do you not say, 'Four months more and then the harvest'? I tell you, open your eyes and look at the fields. They are ripe for harvest"* (Jn 4:35).

☙☙

Some years ago I was diagnosed with breast cancer. During my recovery from a mastectomy I went through waves of fear and depression. On my last night in the hospital, when I was trying to sleep, I sensed the Lord saying to me "I want you to pray with the man in the next room." Filled with self-pity, I rolled over in bed and responded, "Why don't you send someone to pray with me instead?" (A number of people had already prayed with me.) He repeated his request, more insistent than before. Finally, after tossing and turning in bed unable to sleep, I got up.

He was a nice looking black man in his thirties, with a bandage over his eyes. I tiptoed into the room in my robe and slippers and leaned over his bed. "God sent me to pray for you," I whispered awkwardly. I had been trained in hospital visitation ministry and knew this was *not* a recommended approach!

Tears rolled down his cheeks. "Today I gave my life to the Lord," he whispered, "and today I learned that I would never see again. You can't know how much your coming in here means to me." I was overwhelmed, ashamed and deeply humbled. I don't remember my exact prayer, but it stumbled out of a repentant heart and probably went something like this: "Lord, thank you for bringing me here. Please touch his hurt and trauma and bring your highest good." The presence of Jesus was so strong in the room that I don't think I could have said anything more.

In my room I fell to my knees and cried, "Lord, I'm so sorry for my selfishness." After years of living a Christian life and experiencing the blessing of others praying with me on many occasions, I was ashamed to admit that sometimes I was still self-centered. "I don't know how much more time I have left in this life," I cried. "I know breast cancer is unpredictable. But I make a decision to make every moment count in the kingdom of God. I will not waste the precious time you have given me. With your grace I will always say 'Yes, Lord,' when you ask me to pray with someone."

As I reflect back on the years that have passed since that time in the hospital, it is with gratitude for the many opportunities the Lord has given me to pray with people. Most have been little moments, "5-minute miracles," impromptu mini-prayers "on the road." Each experience has been life-giving for me, and I believe also for those receiving prayer. Jesus says, "Give and it shall be given to you..." (Lk 6:38). He knows that our need to pray with others is as great as the need of those with whom we pray.

There is so much hopelessness in the world. We read about it in the daily news and hear it in the workplace. What drives people to hurt each other in such terrible ways? Why do people end up helpless and homeless and desperate? Why is society so out of control? Oh, Lord, have mercy.

Sometimes the hopelessness is so overwhelming that I block it from my mind. Recently while a friend and I were walking down a San Francisco street we passed a beggar on a corner. My friend looked at him with gentle eyes, gave him an encouraging word and put a few coins in his little box. I looked the other way. By the time we reached our destination he had done this several times. I wanted to cry. "Watching you," I said, "I realized that sometimes I can't look into the face of despair. I turn away." Somehow his gentle love reached out to them as quiet prayer. As I turned to the Lord in my heart and asked forgiveness, I felt his love encircling all of us — my companion, myself and the various people he had touched on the walk. Jesus was quietly reminding me, "They are all your brothers and sisters."

We can readily see the desperation and hopelessness of

many of the people on our streets and in our jails. Many others are successful at hiding their pain — at least for awhile. Consider the Catholic women's group in a wealthy church where I spoke. As I began to share, the Holy Spirit showed me a vision of those smiling and gracious women, looking perfect on the outside, but all "scrunched down" on the inside. I shared my vision with them. At the end of the meeting a well-dressed young woman came up and whispered, "Will you please pray for me? I'm one of the scrunched down ones." Despair has many faces, not always visible.

For many years I was one of those trying to hide my hopelessness. Over the course of my life I have experienced marriage failure, family mental health issues, early child-hood sexual abuse, breast cancer and many other traumas. My father was an atheist and my mother was too beaten down emotionally to raise her children as Christians. I was a loner with dark secrets, filled with fear and insecurity.

Following the death of my stepson, Randy, I experienced a powerful spiritual conversion. When I entrusted my life into the care of Jesus Christ, I found hope. In the years to follow many people reinforced that hope through concrete expressions of love. I admired them and wanted to be like them.

Nancy taught me a lot about simple ministry to strangers. Her style in revealing the love of Jesus touched me deeply. In a coffee shop, she would include the waitress in our prayers before the meal or give a kind word to the person at the next table. In the car, she would offer a brief healing prayer for a gas station attendant who would spontaneously spill out his troubles to her while pumping gas. It would all happen in a few moments. More than any other person, she encouraged my participation in the mode of prayer that I call "5-minute miracles." And perhaps more than anyone else she helped me recognize the role and power of the Holy Spirit in these 5-minute miracles. It was also Nancy who introduced me to Father Joe Otte. Through his ministry I had many opportunities to reach out beyond my "comfort zone" and pray with others.

One of the first things I learned from both of them was that my own pain and troubles, rather than holding me back from praying with people, could push me forward. My heart began to go out to people who were suffering, especially in areas where I had experienced heartache. And somehow the pain in my life was ministered to by the ones with whom I prayed. So, if there is pain and sorrow in your life, please be encouraged. As you pray with others, you may find some remarkable things happening in your own life.

Why We Hesitate to Pray with Each Other

In my recent travels around the United States and to other countries, I sometimes offer simple, informal workshops on praying with people. We talk about how to prepare, what to say and what not to say. Then we practice on each other. The results have been very encouraging. These workshops evolved because I kept hearing about people's struggles with what to say and how to say it when an opportunity for prayer is presented.

Some people are afraid they will pray and nothing will happen. Rather than raise false hopes or look foolish when there is no apparent change, they do nothing. Sometimes people don't feel like they are good enough. People often say, "Oh, I'm not the expert. Go see so and so. They are the ones who pray with people." Often we don't realize that the Holy Spirit has nudged us to pray because we are exactly the one who can touch a particular person's heart. The right person to pray is usually the one there at the moment, even though someone else may pray again later. We need to remind ourselves that Jesus works through our willingness flowing through our brokenness. It's not our ability or capability, but our availability that counts.

Sometimes hesitation is due to a lack of preparation by the Church for such a vital ministry. Until recently, casual face-to-face prayer has not been a regular part of Church experience. We're not reluctant to say, "I'll be praying for you," but a spontaneous one or two line informal prayer *with* a person is often scary.

Some people hold back because they feel they have to "write a psalm" or compose a perfect prayer before they open their mouth. People sometimes feel there is only one "right way" to pray. Yet having a heart that is right toward God is more important than perfect words. Our personalities and styles will bring the right words. It seems to me that we need to loosen up, relax, pray in a way that is comfortable and ask the Lord to make up the difference.

People are hurting and we can help. We don't have to arrive at a place of perfection before we start exercising the gift of prayer. We don't have to be more than we are. God can use us right now, right where we are. As we say "Yes, Lord," he will give us opportunities to grow in love and service that may have implications throughout eternity. "Then I heard the voice of the Lord saying, 'Whom shall I send? And who will go for us?' And I said, 'Here am I. Send me' " (Is 6:8).

Goal for This Book

From childhood, Catholics are taught that their purpose in life is to know, love and serve God and one another. One of the most effective ways to express our love of God and others is to pray directly with people for their needs. In fact, there is probably no better way to evangelize. Our goal is to develop simple, basic skills in praying with people at the point of need. This is not a training manual to equip people to deal with complex issues in prayer ministry. Upon completion, readers should be able to reach out and pray spontaneously with greater ease.

Each chapter has a theme for deeper reflection: evangelization, empowerment, empathy, service, trust, growth, wisdom and sanctification.

Keep a notebook to record your experiences and to list the prayer requests people will make along the way. Don't forget to leave space for praise reports as they are answered. It won't be long before you will see amazing changes in others and in your own life. There are many 5-minute miracles on the way!

KEY POINTS

- The world is full of hurting people.
- A life entrusted into the care of Jesus Christ finds hope.
- Hope can be reinforced through concrete expressions of love.
- Our own pain can motivate us to pray with others.
- As we pray with others we receive blessings.

EXERCISES

1. Ask God in prayer to reveal to you what you find hard about praying with people and ask him to heal it.

2. Daily bring the situation to God and ask him to continue to move in it so you are no longer afraid.

☯☯

Lord, give me a gift of evangelization. Open my eyes, my heart, my hands, my ears, my will to the needs of others. Give me a zeal to reach and touch others with your healing love. Thank you, Lord. Amen.

2

The Holy Spirit Our Enabler

" ... the Holy Spirit, who sanctifies the people of God through the ministry and sacraments gives to the faithful special gifts as well (cf. 1 Cor 12:7), 'allotting to everyone according to his will' (1 Cor 12:11). Thus may the individual, 'according to the gift each has received, administer it to one another' and become 'good stewards of the manifold grace of God' (1 Pet 4:10) and build up thereby the whole body in charity (cf. Eph 4:16)."

—Documents of Vatican II, Decree on
the Apostolate of the Laity, chapter 1, paragraph 3

Theme: EMPOWERMENT (to enable; provide with means or opportunity; make possible; to make me able to do something): " ... *you will receive power when the Holy Spirit comes on you; and you will be my witnesses ... to the ends of the earth"* (Acts 1:8).

☙

Although I converted to the Catholic faith many years ago, it was not a heart conversion until after the death of my stepson. A few days after Randy's funeral, in utter despair, I turned on the television. A Christian evangelist was just beginning to pray a prayer of surrender. Falling to my knees I prayed with him:

"Jesus, I am sorry for the things I have done that offended you. I repent of my sins. I turn away from them and turn to you. Please come into my heart and be the Lord of my life. I receive you as my Lord and Savior. Please fill me with your Holy Spirit. Thank you Jesus. Amen."

That was truly for me a 5-minute miracle — the biggest of my life! My love for the Christian community and the Church began to blossom. Suddenly I yearned for friends. My first prayer, "Lord, give me friends," was answered a thousand fold.

One morning in church I literally fell into the arms of a total stranger. Mary Augusta took me home for coffee, conversation and informal prayer. Starting slowly, I tested this thing called friendship. After telling her a few things about my life I would watch to see if she still loved me. She would hug me, cry with me, share some of her own pain and the way Jesus helped her through the pain. Then she would pray a simple healing prayer. There came a time when she knew everything about me, and I knew she still loved me. Something deep inside was healed through my relationship with Mary Augusta. The time together was healing for both of us.

When I prayed the prayer of surrender, I yielded my life into the care of Jesus and asked for the release of the Holy Spirit, promised to those who ask: " ... how much more will your Father in heaven give the Holy Spirit to those who ask him" (Lk 11:13). The first thing that happened was a yearning for community and a love of people. Secondly, I was drawn to scripture. I would spend endless hours reading the Bible. It came alive for me. My mind was being cleansed and transformed by the word of God. Deep areas of my life began to be healed as they were being washed with the love of Jesus. I was coming to life.

Next, I became aware of an increasingly sensitized conscience. The things I could get away with before, I could no longer do comfortably. Bad attitudes, immoral thoughts, bitterness, unforgiveness, lying — things like this began to offend my spirit. I yearned to be around like-minded people, to sing, to praise and to pray. They became my extended family.

Training Centers for 5-Minute Miracles

Mary Augusta introduced me to prayer meetings, which soon became an important part of my life. During a Life in the Spirit Seminar we prayed for a Pentecost experience as in the Book of Acts — when the Holy Spirit filled the apostles and empowered them to witness to the world through preaching and healing. We learned that the same Spirit enabled us to do wondrous things for God.

Early on, I learned that the Holy Spirit was our intercessor, helping us in prayer: "...the Spirit helps us in our weakness. We do not know what we ought to pray, but the Spirit himself intercedes for us with groans that words cannot express. And he who searches hearts knows the mind of the Spirit, because the Spirit intercedes for the saints in accordance with God's will" (Rom 8:26–27). Thank you, Jesus, for the gift of your Spirit!

In these gatherings of praise and worship I observed all kinds of healings resulting from simple prayer to the Father, through the Son, in the power of the Holy Spirit. A person would come with a need; one or more persons would gather and pray a simple prayer, committing the situation into our Heavenly Father's hands. Sick people would often be healed or greatly improved. Sometimes the one praying would be impressed to share a word with the individual receiving prayer that brought release from a burden. Sometimes the power of God would be so strong that those receiving prayer would enter into a deep rest. People often received deep physical, emotional and spiritual healing in those encounters with the Holy Spirit.

Newcomers would be amazed. They would watch, listen, learn, then be invited to participate. In gatherings that encouraged such informal prayer, shy and untrained people were being trained and reaching out to pray with others — even outside the prayer group. Prayer meetings can be powerful training centers to develop people in a ministry of 5-minute miracles.

Listening to God

When praying with people, we were trained to listen with two ears: one to God and one to the person. Often the question arises, "How do I hear God?" "How does he speak to me?" Many times I hear, "What do you mean, God spoke to you?"

Think about it this way: He is the still quiet voice in our hearts. He is in the thoughts that the Holy Spirit prompts us to think. It's no more complicated than that. Some people describe it as, "the thought came to me," or "the idea popped into my mind." Others link it to the voice of conscience, mentioned in the Documents of Vatican II: "In the depths of his conscience, man detects a law which he does not impose on himself, but which holds him in obedience. Always summoning him to love good and avoid evil, the voice of conscience can when necessary speak to his heart more specifically: do this, shun that. For man has in his heart a law written by God" (Documents of Vatican II, Pastoral Constitution on the Church in the Modern World, Chapter 1, paragraph 16).

As we reach out to pray with others, Jesus will guide us in a variety of ways: thoughts or sentences in the heart, scriptures that 'come alive,' impressions, nudges, urges, feelings. He speaks in many ways.

A situation of 'hearing' God through non-verbal communication is illustrated in the following story. When a friend and I were driving to her family's summer cabin, I felt an unexplainable urge to pray as we drove. After about an hour on the road my friend developed a desire to stop along the way to make a purchase at a particular men's store. When I talked to the clerk as he gift-wrapped her purchase, I learned he was an ex-priest. Impetuously I asked, "What did you do, leave to get married?" When I learned he had never married, my spirit was stirred to ask, "Why don't you go back?" He admitted that my question confirmed a deep longing in his heart. Then I asked, "Could we pray in the car before we leave?" He agreed. The three of us sat in the car and joined hands as I prayed simply: "Lord, you have a plan for Bob's life. We intercede for your perfect plan to be realized. We thank you and praise you for the gift of this time. Amen." After the prayer we simply sat in silence enjoying God's presence that came, as soon as we started to pray. Many wonderful changes have occurred in this man's life since that moment of prayer in the car in a shopping center parking lot. For me, this was a wonderful example of a 5-minute miracle.

The way we 'heard' the Lord throughout the encounter was through nudges and tugs and senses and feelings and urges, rather than audible words from the Lord. Looking back, we saw the action of the Lord through all the steps, from the initial urge to pray to the last minute decision to give Bob a copy of a prayer booklet that contained my phone number. It provided a means for later contact.

"How do we know what we hear is from the Lord?" This question was asked during a workshop in Arizona. The following response was offered by another participant: "It's like recognizing a close friend's presence. When a friend comes into the room, even when you don't physically see the person, there is a uniquely familiar atmosphere. So it is with the Lord." Jesus says in John 10:4, "His sheep follow him because they know his voice." When we spend time with him in intimate fellowship we come to know his voice and presence. That knowledge will grow as the relationship grows. Often while meditating on scripture or sitting quietly in prayer, a word of encouragement will settle into the mind. Keep a notebook handy to write down these impressions and reflect on them later.

When Jesus speaks, the words or impressions will express love, not condemnation. They will carry a message of comfort, encouragement or inspiration. Even a correction will have a hug in it.

We all know that not everything coming into our minds is from the Lord. The more intimate we become with Jesus through our prayer and reflection in scripture, the more we recognize which thoughts are the nature and character of Jesus. "...they will never follow a stranger; in fact they will run away from him because they do not recognize a stranger's voice" (Jn 10:5).

The topic is far deeper than this, but for now just be encouraged. As we begin to reach out to others in prayer, the Holy Spirit will help us in a wonderful variety of ways, especially giving words of healing, hope and encouragement for those in need.

Gifts that Release 5-Minute Miracles

The Holy Spirit gives gifts of service listed in 1 Corinthians 12: tongues, prophecy, interpretation of tongues, word of knowledge, wisdom, faith, healing and miracles. The commonly referred to gifts in Isaiah 11:2 (wisdom and understanding, counsel and might, knowledge and the fear of the Lord) are directed primarily toward personal sanctification. When we surrender to Jesus as Lord, his whole nature is available to us. The gifts listed above are some of the aspects of the nature of Jesus, who lives in us. Whenever I pray with someone, I ask the Lord to release those service gifts necessary to accomplish his highest purposes at that time.

The gift of tongues as a prayer language has been helpful to me in personal prayer and in praying with people. To help understand this gift, there is a humorous story about a friend who was telling the Lord as he was getting ready for work one morning, that he wanted any gift but tongues. As he stood in the bathroom brushing his teeth, he heard (in his heart) the Lord saying, "I've been talking to you all these years in your language. Won't you talk to me now in mine?" My friend laughed, then cried, and something deep inside was released. He began praying in tongues — with toothpaste running down his cheek.

In some mysterious way tongues seems to be the Lord's special spiritual language, uniquely different for each of us, yet drawing us into an intimacy and openness of spirit that allows other gifts to emerge. It's not something learned or earned, but a gift we can ask for and yield to, and which grows with use.

The 'word of knowledge' is a wonderful gift in praying with people. Sometimes as we pray with people we may hear in our hearts a word like "forgiveness" or "brother," etc. The Lord may be telling us the person needs to forgive, or there is healing needed with a brother. When that happens, ask the Lord for his wisdom to handle it. All of the service gifts are for healing people and restoring lives.

As we yield our lives to the management of the Holy Spirit he brings the enlightment of Jesus into our spirits, helps us understand ourselves, shows us how to live and empowers us to serve others. The more we surrender, the more he is able to empower us to serve.

KEY POINTS

- In surrendering to Jesus our lives begin to open to others.

- In prayer groups we often find opportunities to grow in our ability to pray with others.

- Spending time with Jesus helps us to know his voice and presence.

- As we reach out to pray with others the Holy Spirit helps with various gifts.

- The service gifts are for healing people and restoring lives.

EXERCISES

1. Reflect daily on the great love God has for you until you accept that as true in your own life.

2. Ask Jesus to send his Holy Spirit upon you as he did with the apostles at Pentecost and has done with people throughout the ages.

∾

Heavenly Father, thank you for my life. Thank you for the grace to surrender to you. Thank you for stirring in me a desire to give. Loving Father, I need your power in my life. Melt me, mold me, fill me, use me. Release your gifts of service and the insight to use them with wisdom and love. Thank you for creating opportunities to serve your people in a way that glorifies you. In Jesus' name I pray. Amen.

3

Prayer of Preparation

"Since the works of charity and mercy afford the most striking testimony of the Christian life, apostolic formation should lead also to the performance of these works so that the faithful may learn from childhood to have compassion for their brothers and to be generous in helping those in need."

—Documents of Vatican II, Decree on
the Apostolate of the Laity, chapter 6, paragraph 31

Theme: EMPATHY (capacity for participation in another's feelings; sympathy; compassion): *" . . . a Samaritan, as he traveled, came where the man was; and when he saw him, he took pity on him. He went to him and bandaged his wounds, pouring on oil and wine. Then he put the man on his donkey, took him to an inn and took care of him"* (Lk 10:33–34).

☙

Someone asked a friend of mine, "Why do you have so many opportunities to pray with people during the day? It never happens to me." My friend responded, "Because I ask the Lord to send people to me. Do you?" The person said, "No. I never thought of asking."

We can begin each day by asking the Lord to send people needing prayer to us:

"Lord, I offer this day to you. Please bring a hurting person to me today and give me the grace, wisdom and courage to recognize and respond to their needs in a way that glorifies you. Please prepare both of us for this time. Open the door and create the opportunity for us to pray. Thank you, Lord. Amen."

When I travel on speaking engagements one of the ways I prepare is to ask Jesus to connect me with the hearts of the people. One day a priest celebrating Mass at one of my services told the people I was "one of the most non-threatening guest speaker he had heard!" Let's ask the Lord to create around us a sense of being warm and safe and "non-threatening," so that people receiving prayer can let down their guard and relax. Try visualizing your heart going out and drawing people in to where Jesus lives inside. This creates a warm atmosphere and can happen even at a grocery check-out stand, on a coffee break or over the phone.

Pray with a Partner

There is great value in praying with a partner. Some of the benefits include: increased power, protection and discernment. The Lord sent the apostles out two by two. When I pray with my prayer partner, Barbara, we make a point to clear the air ahead of time. Because we have different styles and personalities, it is easy to get on each other's nerves. So as we head out to pray with someone, we ask each other, "Do you have anything against me?" And then we work it through. When our unity is restored we are able to pray for the person.

The key is to somehow get beyond personalities to see others as Jesus sees them. One time when I was ill, the Lord sent someone to pray with me that I previously avoided because of their abrasive personality. I was healed! Jesus was teaching me an important lesson!

There is great power in united prayer. As we continue to let down the walls, we will begin to see more and more miracles.

Another lesson on preparation can be learned from my mother's experience with dad. She struggled for 50 years in a difficult marriage, praying continually, "Lord, teach me to love." One day when she wanted to pack up and leave, the Lord said, "You have to learn it sometime. It might as well be now." This is what he said to her: "You can't do it on your own strength. Do you want to love your husband? Love him with my love. Do you need to forgive? Take my forgiveness. All my resources are available to you because I live in you to be your ability." What followed was many years of entering into the life of Jesus that was available from God's spirit.

The key is to remember to pray: "Lord, I can't do it. Please do it through me." This is true as we pray for our own needs or the needs of others. Surrendered and humble, with our eyes on Jesus, we can pray:

"Lord, I can't heal your people. Heal them through me. I can't love. Love through me. I can't bring change. Make me an instrument of change. I can't reach this person. Reach them through me."

This is the secret of miracle power.

KEY POINTS

- Many people begin each day by asking God to send people who need prayer to them.

- Create a warm atmosphere so people can let down their guard and relax.

- Praying in unity with a partner is powerful and effective.

- Prayer of preparation centers us on Jesus and opens us to be vessels of healing for others.

- The key is to remember Jesus does the work through us.

EXERCISES

1. Remember that your relationship with Jesus is your best preparation. Pray for a docility to his nature.

2. Reflect on God's great love rather than the problem. God can speak from his love.

☙❧

Loving Heavenly Father, I come to you through the blood of the Lord Jesus Christ in praise and worship and adoration.

Empty me now of anything that would interfere with your purpose — everything of the flesh, world or evil one. Thank you for sending the Holy Spirit to empower and guide me in communicating your love. Help me to express your love in a way that can bring us both into a new awareness of your presence in our lives. Thank you for releasing the specific gifts of service necessary to accomplish your purposes. Thank You, Jesus, for promising to be with us when we gather in your name. Your desire for our wholeness is even greater than our own. Be glorified in our lives and our time together. Amen.

☯

PRAYER OF ST. FRANCIS

Lord, make me an instrument of your peace.
Where there is hatred, let me sow love.
Where there is injury, forgiveness.
Where there are doubts, faith.
Where there is darkness, light.
Where there is sadness, joy.

O divine Master,
grant that I may not so much seek
to be consoled as to console;
to be understood as to understand;
to be loved as to love.
For it is in giving that we receive;
it is in pardoning that we are pardoned;
and it is in dying that we are born to eternal life.

4

What Do We Say When We Pray?

"This most sacred Council, then, earnestly entreats in the Lord that all laymen give a glad, generous and prompt response to the voice of Christ, who is giving them an especially urgent invitation at this moment, and to the impulse of the Holy Spirit."

—Documents of Vatican II, Decree on
the Apostolate of the Laity, Chapter 6, paragraph 33

Theme: SERVICE (to attend to another's needs; performing duties for another; to help): "... *serve one another in love*" (Gal 5:13).

☙☙

Picture yourself in a conversation with a co-worker, perhaps during a coffee break or during your lunch hour. The person admits being burdened with a personal need. Be aware of the Holy Spirit drawing you to respond in some way. Silently pray a prayer of preparation, then suggest: "Could we pray and ask Jesus to help?"

Touch is an important part of sharing God's love. If it's possible, a gentle hand on the shoulder or on the hand of a person expresses your coming together before God in a caring way. If it's a public place the person can be put at ease by the words, "The others will think we are just talking." Keep it simple as in any normal conversation:

"Lord, show us how to pray. Thank you for your love and your light. Bring your peace and your healing into this situation. We know that nothing is impossible for you and we thank you for moving in this area of concern right now. Amen."

Sometimes the prayer may be simply, "Lord, you know this person's problem. Please take care of it." Sometimes it helps to see ourselves coming as little children trusting a loving daddy to fix a hurt. It doesn't have to be any more profound than that. Prayer is conversation with God, so let it be as natural as asking a friend a favor: "Lord, help us." The important thing is that you are coming together in God's presence and making requests. "Do not be anxious about anything, but in everything, by prayer and petition, with thanksgiving, present your requests to God" (Phil 4:6).

The Lord may give you something else to say or even a mental picture or impression. Ask him if he wants you to share it or just pray about it silently. If you received an impression of fear in the other person, for example, you might say gently, "I have a sense that there may be some fear. Is this true?" If so, you might pray, "Jesus, please go into the root cause of the fear. Thank you for pouring your healing love into the center of the fear." (When praying I often find myself thanking him more than asking him, because he is always moving us toward wholeness.)

There may be an impression of a broken heart. Again, you might say, "I have a sense that in some way your heart has been broken. May I pray about that?" You could gently pray for the Lord to touch and heal the root cause of the broken heart and to pour in his love.

Once when I was doing a workshop on praying with people, I asked for a volunteer to demonstrate. While praying with her in front of the group I received an image in my mind of a green field with a fence down the middle. After describing what I saw, I asked if it meant something to her. She responded, "There is division in my family." Then I asked, "May I pray about that situation?" With her agreement, I asked the Lord to break down any dividing wall of hostility in her family (Eph. 2:17) and restore unity and peace. Note that I did not try to explain the vision for her, but left it to her own interpretation.

During prayer I generally ask the Lord to heal root causes, not just the symptoms, and to bring wholeness to body, mind and spirit. The person is encouraged to give God permission to enter the circumstances and to face and deal with obstacles that block the Lord's healing love.

The prayer time could close something like this: "Lord, I thank you and praise you for your love and all you are doing and will continue to do in each of our lives. Amen."

In some circumstances it is helpful to ask the person for feedback: "What happened inside when we prayed? Were you comfortable with the prayer?" Both can learn from the response.

Prayers Cradled in Love

One time I was sitting in a coffee shop talking to a friend about some troubled areas of my life. During a pause in the conversation she reached over, took my hand and asked simply, "May I pray for you — right now?" I was overwhelmed by the love and compassion in her voice. In the next few minutes she simply lifted to the Lord the areas of need I had expressed, and then prayed quietly. It wasn't so much the words she spoke, but that they were cradled in love, that touched me so deeply. After a moment of silence she said gently, "I sense the Lord wants to heal some insecurity in your life. May I pray about that also?" I nodded, adding, "Insecurity has always been an issue in my life." She prayed for the Lord to touch the root cause of my insecurity and to pour in his healing love and strength. The prayer didn't last more than a few minutes, but the effects have been ongoing.

Nancy and the Department Store Clerk

Nancy was standing at a variety store check out counter one day, paying for a purchase and making light conversation with the youthful cashier. As he handed her the change she simply said, "Bless him, Lord." In that statement he felt her acceptance of him as a person. Perhaps he was "scrunched down" and the "Bless him, Lord" lifted him up. He then admitted it had been a while since he'd been to church. "What I'd really appreciate," he said, "is for you to pray for a girl I like. She won't pay any attention to me." So she prayed out loud in his presence, "Lord, touch her heart and open the communication for your best purposes to be accomplished." As Nancy walked away he smiled and said, "I think I'll invite her to the church play." He had strayed from church and in that brief encounter he began an inner movement back toward God.

Betty's account of her experiences with Ben is filled with wisdom and hope. We can learn much through studying the story.

Jesus and Ben

"I kept running into Ben in the Safeway Market. He would tease me about being a Catholic holy roller and I would tease him about always sitting in the back row at daily Mass. He said, "No, I can't sit closer. I might get zapped." One day he said, "I have gout. Don't pray for me but think about me. I have to get rid of it." I said, "Okay, I will pray for God to show you some way to get rid of it." That afternoon when I picked up a magazine I saw an article about eating cherries for gout. I tore out the page and carried it in my purse until I saw him at the market a few days later. Handing it to him I said, "I think God answered your prayer." He said, "I'll try it." As I turned to continue on my way I said, "I prayed over the paper. Let me know how it works."

He was always afraid something of God would touch him, yet he couldn't let go of contact with me. Three days later in the market he said, "It's a pretty good remedy. It did help." Smiling, I said, "Of course I prayed for you too." He shook his head, saying, "The article said nothing about God." Continuing, I said, "You can't really hold anything against God, I see you at daily Mass." "Well, I respect him," was his response.

Three weeks later it was announced at Mass that "the man who comes here daily had a stroke." They didn't know his name, but I knew it was Ben. Finally an older couple mentioned he had been moved to a convalescent hospital in Concord, probably to die. Nobody knew which hospital. I said, "Oh Lord, no one knows where he is or anything about him, but he is heavy on my heart. Tell me how to find him and when to see him."

One morning after Mass the Lord said, "This is the time." Someone at Mass said he might be at Bayview Hospital in Concord. Praying all the while, I took the first freeway exit into town and immediately saw the hospital. At the front desk I asked for "a man named Ben in a coma who had been there four days." They took me directly to him.

Touching his hand, I identified myself as Betty, the lady he teased at Safeway. There was no response. "I've come to talk to you about something very important," I said gently. "I know you love Jesus. I want to remind you of something, because you now have to make a decision which way you want to go. You may want to stay here on earth if you feel you have unfinished responsibilities. Recognizing God's love, you also may feel a drawing to go home. I don't want you to be afraid. If you believe in Jesus, believe that he took the punishment for your sins. If you believe Jesus died for your sins you have nothing to worry about. I know you believe in Jesus so you are free. Don't be afraid, because God wants to love you at home as well as on earth. You need to make a choice." There was still no response.

Continuing, I said, "I'm going to pray in that pentecostal stuff (tongues) under my breath so you won't be worried, but my hand is on your arm so you will know I am still here." I prayed a few moments and then said, "I know how much Jesus has loved you and how much you have wanted to love him. He loves you any way you come to him." At that moment, tears came to his eyes and he formed with his mouth the words, "Thank you."

Ben died two hours later. I explained to a priest who knew I had been with him that I had presented the salvation plan in words Ben could understand. A few days later when I spoke with relatives who arrived from Ireland, they told me that his family had totally rejected him. It seemed like no one cared if he lived or died."

Let's ask the Lord to anoint us with a spirit of adventure for just such encounters. They are surely more precious than gold. "Let us then approach the throne of grace with confidence, so that we may receive mercy and find grace to help us in our time of need" (Heb 4:1).

KEY POINTS

- Touch can express coming together before God in a caring way.

- Keep the words simple as in normal conversation.

- Prayer is simply coming together in God's presence and presenting requests.

- Ask Jesus to heal root causes and bring wholeness.

- Ask the person to give God permission to enter the circumstances and face and deal with obstacles.

EXERCISES

1. Ask the Holy Spirit to send you people so you can practice.

2. As you pray, remember your willingness to be vulnerable is the doorway to God's love.

◎◎

Lord Jesus, please touch anything in my heart that would hold me back from praying with people. Give me courage, wisdom and perseverance. Thank you, Lord. Amen.

5

What Comes after the Prayer?

"Giving the body unity through himself and through his power and through the internal cohesion of its members, this same Spirit produces and urges love among the believers."

—Documents of Vatican II, Dogmatic Constitution
on the Church, chapter 1, paragraph 7

Theme: TRUST (assured reliance on the character, ability, strength and truth of another; place confidence in; believe in): *"Trust in the Lord with all your heart and lean not on your own understanding"* (Prov 3:5).

☙

After 40 years of marriage my dad ran away and left my mom. A few weeks after he left, the Lord asked mom what she really wanted in life. It was a profound moment. Upon deep reflection, she responded, "I *really want* a marriage." She made her desire known and rested it in the Lord's hands. She did not try to drag her husband home. It was a time of total surrender and trust.

In prayer we make our desires known to the Lord and surrender the results to him. By doing this our hearts are saying, "I love you, Jesus, and I trust in you." In the following family crisis my niece and I had an opportunity to exercise that trust.

When my brother-in-law, Harvell, was killed in a plane crash in the Caribbean, the family was devastated. As we gathered at his home in Colorado, his oldest daughter, Lori, told the family that she wanted to see her father's body. Everyone was afraid that she couldn't handle the shock, as he had died of head injuries. Yet she was an adult and had a right to make her own decision.

On the night before the funeral this choice was being discussed by the family. Lori stated her wishes and walked outside in the dark. I followed her. We stood together silently for a long moment. She knew I loved her very much, and she felt safe with me. That's why I could ask, "Lori, could we ask Jesus what he wants you to do? If he wants you to see your daddy's body, I know he will give you the strength. And if he doesn't want you to ... would you entrust the decision to him?" Her eyes filled with tears as she gave me permission to pray. "Jesus," I prayed simply, "please tell Lori what you would like her to do." Then I went inside, entrusting the results to the Lord. In my heart there was a deep confidence that Jesus would speak to Lori.

When she came inside I could see that something was different about her. There was a certain strength in her, a courage, a radiance, that was new. She leaned over and whispered, "Aunt Linda, Jesus spoke to me." "What did he say?" I asked quietly. These were the words Jesus spoke to her broken heart: "Honey, your daddy wouldn't want you to see him like that." Lori continued, "It's okay, Aunt Linda. I'm okay. I can handle it now." And I knew she could. That moment, in all of its pain, was pure gold. "The Lord is close to the brokenhearted and saves those who are crushed in spirit" (Ps 34:18).

When a friend read this story she said, "This is a wonderful example of what happens after we pray. Your prayer and faith gave your niece the courage to trust that God would talk to her too, and the courage to listen to God speak to her. That's exactly what should happen after we pray; that whoever we pray with has the increased faith and courage to pray themselves."

When we are praying with someone going through hard times, we need to remind ourselves that we aren't there to solve the problem, but to help bring Jesus into the center of it. We are intercessors, presenting their needs and concerns to God, whether we pray *with* them at the moment or *for* them at a later time. Later, when these people come to mind, just say silently something like this: "Thank you, Father, for the work you are doing and will continue to do in their lives."

When mom made her request known and surrendered it to the Lord, she did not insist on a particular outcome. In fact, dad returned home and eventually accepted Jesus as Lord. Yet even if she had remained alone for the rest of her life, it would have been simply a call to deeper trust and a call to praise Jesus in everything, no matter what the circumstances.

Most of the time we will never know the outcome of our brief prayers with people in need, but we will know the

Lord's pleasure by a gentle, sweet hug of heaven, now and in eternity. Is there any opportunity in life more precious than standing beside someone and lifting their needs to our loving Father? This experience is high on my list of life's finest moments.

KEY POINTS

- Entrust the results to the Lord.

- Our prayer and faith give others the courage to trust God to speak and courage to listen.

- We are there to help bring Jesus into the center of the problem.

- We may never know the outcome of our prayers.

- Praying for others can be high on the list of golden moments in life.

EXERCISE

1. When the remembrance of a person prayed for comes to you, thank God for his faithfulness and tender love.

2. If the remembrance continues, ask the Lord if there is more prayer he wants you to do for the person or situation.

☺☺

Lord Jesus, please reveal any area in my life where I do not trust you. Please come into that area and heal it, that I may trust you more fully than ever before. Thank you, Lord. Amen.

6

Suggestions for Family Prayer

"The family has received from God its mission to be the first and vital cell of society. It will fulfill this mission if it shows itself to be the domestic sanctuary of the Church through the mutual affection of its members and the common prayer they offer to God ... "

—Documents of Vatican II, Decree on
the Apostolate of the Laity, chapter 3, paragraph 11

Theme: GROWTH (movement toward maturity): "*... grow in the grace and knowledge of our Lord and Savior Jesus Christ ... "* (2 Pet 3:18).

◎◎

When I was a young woman I would cry when I witnessed fathers praying with families. It touched me deeply. There was only one time my dad prayed with me. He wasn't even a Christian at the time. It was in the evening, we were alone in the car and I had a headache. Turning to him I asked, "Would you put your hand on my head and ask Jesus to take away my headache?" He put his rough carpenter's hand on my head and said, faithlessly, "Jesus, take away my headache." He didn't even say the words right, but *my* headache left.

My favorite time praying with mom happened about a year after dad died. We were drinking coffee in the kitchen of mother's little cottage near the central Oregon coast. It was a new environment for mom, a major change from her home with dad in San Diego, California. She hunched down a little as she said awkwardly, "The truth of the matter is, all of my life I've been afraid of the dark." Her confession brought tears to my eyes, as this was not something I had known about her. "When your father was alive I could handle it. But now he's gone, and I have to face the fear alone."

My sister and I encircled her in a hug prayer, asking Jesus to go into the root cause of her fear of the dark and send his healing light. We asked the Lord to take away all fear and pour in his healing love. "There is no fear in love. But perfect love casts out fear . . . " (1 Jn 4:18). Then we passed around a box of tissues to dry our eyes. It was one of the most precious moments with my mother I have ever known.

There is an old saying, "Families that pray together stay together." I believe it is also true that families praying together can help heal each other. Yet what I continually hear is how hard it is to pray with family members — much harder than with friends or with a prayer group or even strangers.

There are enormous benefits when we persevere in prayer for our family. For that reason I wanted to share a few ideas from people who have been able to successfully pray with their family.

Overcoming Resistance

One friend shared, "Before my husband was open to prayer I would pray for him silently as I hugged him before he set off to work. After he would fall asleep I would lay my hand upon him and pray for an openness to the Holy Spirit and an openness to healing deep in his heart." Her husband is now very receptive to family prayer. About her children she shared, "Often when I see resentment or hardness in my children I will go to them after they have fallen asleep and pray over them. I see a noticeable change in a day or two. When I encourage my family to pray with me, I let them know in a light-hearted way that I need their prayers. If we don't pray as a family I feel it's like putting them out in the rain without an umbrella. And, even though my twelve-year-old rolls her eyes, I continue to share with her our answered prayers. I don't get discouraged by her reaction because I know her spirit is hearing every word."

For those with difficulty verbalizing prayer one suggestion is to have each person write prayer requests on a piece of paper. Exchange papers and pray out loud for the other's needs. As it becomes easier, each can begin verbalizing their needs for the other to pray.

Regularity in Prayer

A Canadian friend, Maria, who owns businesses with her father in a shopping mall, always meets him for coffee and morning prayers before the day begins. They sit in the food court of the mall and ask a blessing and guidance for the day, taking not more than a couple of minutes in addition to coffee time. She similarly visited her 90-year-old grandfather almost every Saturday night for the last few years of his life, praying a brief prayer with him each time. Her bonding with him went so deep because of those regular but brief visits, that after his death she felt no desire for any of his belongings. Physical possessions couldn't touch what she had already received in her heart. Regularity in family prayer, however brief, can bring lasting rewards.

One young family prays traditional prayers of the Church each night with their 13-year-old twin boys and 8-year-old daughter. They say it is no simple feat, but they found that by keeping a family prayer request journal and allowing the children to take turns voicing these requests and hearing of answered prayers the children are really participating.

A mother in Canada shared with me that she assigns one day a week to each member of her family. Monday belongs to Susie, Tuesday to Dan, etc. Each knows it is their special day. If that format could be combined with praying *with* Susie on Monday for a special need (even on the phone), and *with* Dan on Tuesday, etc., it would be even more powerful.

Another family has a regular "forgiveness night." They gather in a circle in the living room with a chair in the center. One person will sit on the chair and ask forgiveness of someone he has hurt. A child might say to a sibling, "I'm sorry I broke your toy." Forgiveness is expressed, and the person is affirmed and prayed with. Then another family member sits in the forgiveness chair.

Another family has regular "help" nights. They gather and one at a time say, "This is what I need help with." The word "help" has become a signal in the family, for others to encourage them to express something difficult to communicate.

A friend has a painting of Jesus with his hands outstretched. Family members stick post-it notes with prayer requests on the hands. The notes are taken down and prayed during family prayer time and returned to his hands until the answer comes.

Some married couples say regular morning and evening prayers with each other. They can be traditional prayers of the church or a spontaneous, "Thank you Lord for this day . . . " Many engaged couples have developed regular patterns of praying with each other for their future life together. Some mothers or fathers stand at the door and pray a brief blessing on family members as they leave for the day. The key is to begin, continue on a regular basis, and if the pattern is interrupted, to start over.

Persistence

Don't give up on resistant family members. My mother prayed for me more than thirty years before I surrendered to Jesus. A friend, Becky, tells of how she lived a wild life for many years, including drug and alcohol use, abortions and multiple marriages. One day after attending a psychological seminar with her company she came home reflecting on the big things of life and decided to take a bath. While she was in the tub, shaving her legs and smoking a marijuana cigarette, the Holy Spirit came like a flood. She was filled with the Holy Spirit. All she could think about was telephoning her Portuguese grandma. Wrapped in a damp towel, she dialed the number. "Grandma, do you know God?" Grandma responded, "Yes, Becky." "Do you really know God?" "Yes, Becky, I really know God." Becky still wasn't satisfied. She dressed and drove two hours to her grandma's house and found her in the living room quietly praying. Becky and grandma hugged each other and cried. Becky knew it was because of her grandmother's persistent prayers that she had the grace to surrender.

Never give up on praying for your family. You may have to pray secretly, you may have to give silent hug prayers, you may have to pray as they sleep, but don't stop. In time, you and they will reap the reward.

KEY POINTS

- Families that pray together can help heal each other.

- It can be harder to pray with family than friends or strangers.

- Regularity in family prayer can bring lasting rewards.

- Silent hug prayers and praying over sleeping children can help reduce resistance.

- Never give up.

EXERCISES

1. Thank God daily for his great love for every family member and his desire for their well-being.

2. Bring specific situations to him each day with confidence in his timing and his love.

֍

Lord Jesus, make me an instrument of healing in my family. Show me areas where I may have created disunity and separation. Touch and heal those areas and make me an instrument of unity and blessing. Tell me when to be silent and when to speak. Thank you, Lord. Amen.

7

Learning from Each Other

" ... wisdom gently attracts the mind of man to a quest
and a love for what is true and good ... "

—Documents of Vatican II, Pastoral Constitution on the Church
in the Modern World, Part 1, Chapter 1, paragraph 15

Theme: WISDOM (ability to discern inner qualities and rela-
tionships; insight; sensible; prudent; able to choose sound
ends and appropriate means): *"If any of you lacks wisdom, he
should ask God, who gives generously to all without finding fault,
and it will be given to him"* (Jas 1:5).

☙

Even though we do the best we can, we must remember we
are growing children. If we practice every day learning to
tie our shoes we will one day do it well. We learn with each
opportunity. The key to maturity is in using opportunities
for growth, rather than giving up. That's how we grow. It's
good to have a prayer partner or spiritual director to help
make full use of those opportunities. The following bits of
wisdom are offered by those who pray and those who have
received prayers. We can learn from each other.

Encouragements

Someone asked me recently if I am always comfortable with praying for healing, even if a person is diagnosed as terminally ill. My answer was "Yes," I will pray for the body to be healed and the soul to be loved, entrusting the results to a loving heavenly Father.

Assure people that Jesus has a plan for their life better than they could ask or imagine. " 'For I know the plans I have for you,' declares the Lord, 'plans to prosper you and not to harm you, plans to give you hope and a future' " (Jer 29:11).

The Lord told a prayer group leader one time that he would send more people as the leaders grew in capacity to receive them in love. Let's ask for that same gift. "May the Lord make your love increase and overflow for each other and for everyone else . . . " (1 Thes 3:12).

If you are deeply moved when praying with someone, don't be afraid to let the person see your tears. Jesus wept in front of the people at the tomb of Lazarus (Jn 11:35).

Our faith rests in God, not in our prayers. " . . . and so your faith and hope are in God" (1 Pet 1:21). From a practical standpoint, there is great freedom in knowing our prayers don't have to be perfect. All my training in hospital visitation ministry warned me against saying "God sent me" to the blind man. Yet God brought great good out of my visit with the man in the hospital when I had the mastectomy. It brings us peace to know we can pray, "Lord, please fix it. Make up the difference between what was accomplished and what you desired to do. Thank you, Lord."

Sharing our personal stories of how Jesus has brought healing in our lives can bring hope and open others to believe God will help them too. In fact, writing the story and giving it to people is a good opener and follow up to prayer. "Go . . . and tell the people the full message of this new life" (Acts 5:20).

Encourage people receiving prayer to reach out and pray for others. It's even okay to ask the person to pray with you.

Practice the prayer of presence. Just being with people in pain, confusion, trauma — being their connection to God in the midst of the storm, with or without words — is deeply healing. Sometimes all that is needed is to just hold the person's hand and say, "Lord, help. I don't know how to pray but we know you will work good in this situation. I trust you to bring a greater good than if it hadn't happened." " . . . we know that in all things God works for the good of those who love him, who have been called according to his purpose" (Rom 8:28).

Remember that most healing is a process. Just because we don't see a final result when we pray, we can trust that Jesus has accomplished what was needed through our prayers.

Other Issues

People need Jesus more than they need our good advice and counsel. Most of us are not trained counselors and our lack of knowledge can cause harm when we go beyond our limits. Our job is to bring people into the presence of Jesus the healer. The Lord may suggest their reading a particular scripture passage or encourage regular prayer meeting attendance. He might prompt you to suggest counseling, or he might have you offer to pray with the person again. The distinction as I understand it is this: Our job is not to solve their problem but to point them to Jesus.

Listen without judgment. The person may say things contrary to your belief. Sometimes a first step of healing for another can be our quiet, non-judgmental listening. The Holy Spirit will make the corrections in his time. We are all in process.

Be careful to identify and respect their comfort zone. If they are uncomfortable with touch, don't touch. If praying in tongues is not a part of their prayer experience, don't pray aloud in tongues (or introduce them to it if there is interest). Just be very sensitive to their differences, even in your choice of words in prayer.

It's important to keep the prayer time private. "Keep safe that which was entrusted to you" (1 Tim 6:20). People receiving prayer need to be able to walk away peacefully, knowing that we respect their privacy and that we won't discuss the matter with anyone without their permission. If we can be a safe place for God's wounded ones, he will entrust more of them to us.

Praying for people with mental health problems is one of the most delicate of all. Consider using few words and a lot of love.

Try to connect the person to a prayer/support group for

ongoing assistance. In times of pain people are usually the most open to receive help.

Stay centered in community, submitted to authority. Be careful to not become a lone ranger.

Better Left Unsaid

Sometimes in our frustration and desire to help, we have attempted to come up with quick-fix comments about complex situations. Some examples include, "Buck up, things will get better." Or, "You're strong, you can handle it." These and exhortations such as, "You just have to have more faith" are better left unsaid.

There's another sensitive area. A woman phoned from another state filled with confusion because people in her local community kept talking about demons while they prayed with her. This is one of the ways Jesus has me handle that matter: We can pray, "Lord, whatever isn't from Jesus that is affecting or afflicting this person — take it away and fill the area with the presence of Jesus." It also occurs to me that if we sense the presence of something evil attacking the person we can silence it under our breath. We don't need to mention it out loud.

We are called to pray, not to be doctors. People who pray with others are generally uncomfortable about saying, "You are healed," even if they feel certain that healing has occurred during prayer. Constrained by love, let's quietly allow the healing to manifest itself. The doctor will confirm it as it comes. Always instruct people to stay on their medicine and follow the doctor's instructions. On the other hand, it is certainly okay to say, "*Be healed* in Jesus' name." Or, we can remind them that healing is a process, and today's step has been taken in their movement toward wholeness.

The Holy Spirit may reveal something about the person's life for intercessory prayer only. Don't always assume that if you see it, you are to say it. Ask for the Lord's wisdom.

Be careful to always pray for God's will to be done in people's lives. Saying to them, for example, "I'm going to pray for you to give up smoking, lose weight, or for your marriage to be restored," without their asking, is being heavy handed. You could pray silently, "Lord, I pray for your highest will to be done in the matter of this person's smoking, weight, marriage, etc." We can pray for God's will because we trust him, knowing he loves these people and wants a much higher good for them than we could even imagine. He will always move us toward wholeness if we pray for his will to be done.

KEY POINTS

- The secret of maturity is in using opportunities for growth.

- Love, listen and share yourself without judgment.

- Respect; don't be doctor; pray for God's will.

- Avoid counseling and quick-fix solutions.

- Point people to Jesus.

EXERCISES

1. Whenever you come from a prayer opportunity, ask the Holy Spirit to review it and teach you. Jot down notes if helpful.
2. Disengage from the situation by entrusting your efforts to the Holy Spirit. God will look after it.

Thank you Lord for all the ways you teach us as your children. Thank you for the grace to take myself lightly and to remember that all is yours. Amen.

8

Keeping Our Eyes on the Prize

"In his goodness and wisdom, God chose to reveal himself and to make known to us the hidden purpose of his will (cf. Eph 1:9) by which through Christ, the Word made flesh, man had access to the Father in the Holy Spirit and comes to share in the divine nature (cf. Eph 2:18, 2 Pet 1:4). Through this revelation, therefore, the invisible God (cf. Col 1:15, 1 Tim 1:17) out of the abundance of his love speaks to men as friends (cf. Ex 33:11, Jn 15:14–15) and lives among them (cf. Bar 3:38), so that he may invite and take them into fellowship with himself."

— Documents of Vatican II, Dogmatic Constitution on Divine Revelation, chapter 1, paragraph 2

Theme: SANCTIFICATION (growing in divine grace): *"May God himself, the God of peace, sanctify you through and through. May your whole spirit, soul and body be kept blameless at the coming of our Lord Jesus Christ. The one who calls you is faithful and he will do it"* (1 Thes 5:23–24).

☙❧

From childhood we are taught that our purpose in life is to know, love and serve God and each other. One of the most effective ways of doing this is by praying with people. Developing simple skills in informal prayer has been a goal of this book.

Within that stated objective is a prayer that Jesus would anoint us for a variety of encounters with people to practice and develop those skills. It is expected that many people would begin to step out in faith to pray that Jesus would heal through them. I pray this is happening for you.

He is forming us into servants of love. It is his ministry, not ours. They are his people, and every act of service is an act of worship. When we serve our brothers and sisters it is Jesus we serve. Everything we do for others, we do for him because he loves them so.

As we meet the blind, the beggars, the scrunched down ones, let's serve them with a heart that remembers how Jesus loves them. As we encounter gas station attendants, clerks in the stores and daughters who have lost their fathers, let us love them with the love of heaven, always remembering Jesus' love for each one and his desire for their wholeness.

As we encounter atheist fathers, fearful mothers, resentful children and resistant husbands and wives, let us remember how precious they are to God and keep our hearts focused on his desire for their well-being.

As we hear about people like Ben, let's be attentive to the possibility that in God's eyes casual connections may have a deeper long term purpose. Let's value each contact, however seemingly superficial, as precious to God.

As our intimacy with Jesus grows, his life in us will begin to overflow into the lives of those for whom we pray. We will come into a place of such union with him that people will be converted and healed by our very presence. All we will have to do is show up — surrendered and obedient — and allow God's Spirit to move. I heard a story about a woman who was praying in church one day. A distraught woman came and sat nearby. After a little while she turned and said, "I've been so unforgiving." They sat in reverent silence, thinking about her words and aware of the presence of God. They prayed together before parting.

Let's return everything we do, perfect and imperfect, to the author and finisher of our faith. Jesus is building his church, and we are his arms and hands and eyes and voice and feet. He calls us to evangelize our communities and empowers us to do exploits for him. He gave us the model of servant as he washed the apostles' feet. He calls us to trust without understanding, promises wisdom when we ask and provides ample opportunities for growth. And, he sanctifies us through and through as we continue in faithful relationship.

Perhaps one day we too, like Father Otte, may "rise to heaven with at least a small army of souls we have touched, inspired to holiness and nudged gently onto the straight and narrow but only safe path of Jesus." " . . . if anyone gives a cup of cold water to one of these little ones because he is my disciple, I tell you the truth, he will certainly not lose his reward" (Mt 10:42).

KEY POINTS

- We are taught that our purpose in life is to know, love and serve God and each other.

- One of the most effective ways to do this is by praying with people.

- Jesus anoints us for healing encounters with his people.

- Every act of service is an act of worship; what we do for others we do for him.

- As our intimacy with him grows, his life in us overflows to others.

EXERCISES

1. Remember that scripture reveals Jesus as he is and wants to live through you.

2. Reflect on Ephesians 4 to see how Jesus wants to live in you.

∾

Thank you, Lord, for choosing me before the world began to be a messenger of hope to those my life touches. Help me to know what that means and to cooperate with your Holy Spirit as I grow in the grace and knowledge of our Lord Jesus Christ. Thank you, Father, for letting me be your child. Amen.

About the Author

LINDA SCHUBERT (pictured in cover photo) was born in Los Angeles, California on November 7, 1937. Although she joined the Catholic Church in 1965, she did not have a heart conversion to Jesus Christ until after her stepson's death in 1977. She came to know the Holy Spirit as her comforter, counselor and best friend, and the one who would bring her into that abundant life in which she chose to live.

Today, Linda is a lay leader in the Catholic Charismatic Renewal in San Jose, California and travels internationally giving teachings, seminars and retreats on prayer of the heart. Since 1985, she has assisted Father Robert DeGrandis, SSJ in writing numerous books, including *Renewed in the Holy Spirit, Coming to Life, Resting in the Spirit, The Gift of Miracles* and the expanded edition of *Healing through the Mass*. Her *Miracle Hour* has sold over 300,000 copies and has been published in Korean, Japanese, Spanish, Hungarian, German, Italian, Chinese and Portuguese.

To order copies of *Miracle Hour* ($2.00 each, plus $1 shipping), or to arrange for a "Miracle Hour or 5-Minute Miracle Workshop" contact Linda Schubert, P.O. Box 4034, Santa Clara, CA 95056 (telephone or fax 408-734-8663).

Published by Resurrection Press